D1525136

Days of Obsidian
Days of Grace

selected poetry and prose
by four Native American writers

Days of Obsidian
Days of Grace

selected poetry and prose
by four Native American writers

Al Hunter

Denise Sweet

Jim Northrup

Adrian C. Louis

Published by Poetry Harbor
Duluth, Minnesota

811.5408
D275

A Poetry Harbor Publication

Copyright 1994

Poetry Harbor
1028 East Sixth Street
Duluth, MN 55805

Cover art, commissioned exclusively for this book, by Walt Bressette. Edited by Patrick McKinnon, Andrea McKinnon and Ellie Schoenfeld. Design and production by Usha Hannigan.

This book was made possible, in part, by a grant from the Arrowhead Regional Arts Council, with funding provided by the Minnesota State Legislature, and by Poetry Harbor Members.

Grateful acknowledgment to the following books and periodicals in which some of this poetry and prose first appeared:

Al Hunter • *North Coast Review*

Jim Northrup • *Walking The Rez Road,* Voyageur Press

Adrian C. Louis • *TriQuarterly, The Southern Review, Caliban, Exquisite Corpse, The Owen Wister Review, Atom Mind, New Letters, Kumquat Meringue, Prairie Winds, Long Shot, Ak:wekon, Poetry Motel, Lactuca, Coffeehouse Quarterly.*

Denise Sweet • *Know By Heart,* Rhiannon Press.

ISBN 0-9641986-0-6 $13.95

Table of Contents

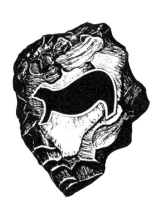

Al Hunter

Manitou Rapids, Ontario

Staying Alive

To be unpredictable
means
to stay alive
through storm and war
to have a mind
unbridled
by horsemen
with whips
for hearts.

Shaman and Black Robe

The catechism of guilt
fails to blend well
with rituals
of faith and forgiveness
I came up through layers
as sap and water
windstorms and rain
Now shifting
between
the power of shamans
and the cold hand
of the cross.

Feast of the Dead

Fall equinox, full moon
What demarcation is this?
Northern lights form an arc
Across the northern sky
At the western edge
Ripple in a chain reaction
Of wave after wave after wave
Of full spectrum colour
To announce your death
Your last song
At your funeral procession
Two eagles showed the way

Tonight the river is a flat plate
Of brilliant colour
And the northern lights
Dance over your grave.

Mishomis

I don't want to live
without the memory of you
I don't want the dream
of tracing the outline of your feet
to end before I die

I dream of your songs
I dream of you singing
I dream of the way your voice sounded
I dream of the way you told the stories
of each song
in the fading light of evening
where they came from
who dreamed them
who taught them to you
when you were young

I haven't forgotten
what you said
When you going to sing
you sing at least four songs eh
When you you going to sing
you go through that song
at least four times eh
at least four times
Don't take no medicine when you sing eh
Once you take that medicine to help you sing
you have to take it all the time after eh
You take it
you have to take it all the time eh

I haven't forgotten
what you said
I have only taken the medicine
of your memory
of your memory
of your memory
of your memory.

Ancestor Poem

Last night the bear was my ancestor
Last night the bear was my memory
trembling at the rustle outside my door

Last night the bear was my ancestor
Last night the bear was my memory
moving through the bushes
frightening me into stone

Last night the bear was my ancestor
Last night the bear was my memory
circling the high rock I stood on
sure there was no safe place

Last night the bear was my ancestor
Last night the bear was my memory
circling through underbrush unseen
breeding remembrance into my body
with every ripple
crushing the underbrush at his feet

Last night the bear was my ancestor
Last night the bear was my memory
returning to heal me
This bear is returning to heal me

Last night the bear was my ancestor
Last night the bear was my memory
speaking with the tenderness of old men

When I heard your voices
calling from four directions
they filled my ears like prayers
Your voices pulled me from my slumber
The pungent sage pulled me near to you

When I came from the north
I saw you praying
your body wrapped in smoke
It was you who called me
to that place on rock
to read the prayers in your body
as it quaked from the fear of me

I saw your feathers shaking
I saw your altar on stone
I saw a shadow like wisps of memory
I saw the years in between

I entered your pipe
when you drew the last breath of it
I filled your body with healing
and did not bruise you.

Anakwad

Cloud.
The one who dreams
his songs
The one who breathes
cedar flute
who wakens birds
to journey
in his sleep
Brother to eagle
beaver and bear
The one who speaks
cedar flute
painted drum
The singing voice
of water
melting ice.

At the Mouth of the Gooseberry River, Three Women

Tineke, Ute, Ellen
the colours of stone
and ice like rippled bone
the sound of ice moving
land pushing mist
we see the edge
of the ice pack
glimpse open water
wonder emerald floor
wonder the dimly lit
underneath, ice ceiling.

In the Sky

He looked down
As though looking down from the very clouds themselves
The down below
Where he first walked
Toward the edge of the wood, fog rolled and lifted
Dew glistened in the meadow
The sun was rising
Onto the shoulders of the eastern sky
He peered down from the clouds
Saw many women dancing
They offered him food
He honoured them with feathers of eagle
He honoured them with songs
They danced the dance of women
Circular, with a side step
Toward the rising sun
In a vision of old and new
They celebrated
There in the meadow, at the edge
Of a green and beautiful wood

A staff of many coloured ribbons
She offered; red, green, yellow and blue
The ribbons were wrapped around a wooden stem
A small hoop at one end
Long leather fringes hanging from the other
A staff of many coloured ribbons she offered
He took what she offered
The wise woman with long grey braids smiled gently
Then left
The coloured ribbons danced
And he lived

He heard the drum songs in his dreams
Sacred voices sounding
He was afraid
He sat at old man's drum
In the light of early evening, singing
He stretched the hide of deer over a new drum
With a younger brother
Stretched the hide of wet skin over the sacred hoop
And celebrated
In a circle they sat, singing
Each pole, each leg, supporting the drum
Represented with four colours
Feathers of eagle staff
Drum pulsing to earth
Gift from a distant star

Rising to the cacophony of the brotherhood of crows
He hears that a brother has fallen
From the branches of earth
Crow laughter spreads
Through the arthritic fingers of bone-bare trees
His story is one that spreads
From the roots of trees
That tells of earth
That spreads up into the heart of layered truths
That spreads out onto the branches
That spreads out onto the arthritic fingers of bone-bare trees
Cacophonic laughter rising
He listens until he is hungry
He rises
A lone deer in the meadow, at dawn, moves slowly
Muzzling green shoots of grass
She is hungry too

He does not know if his dreams are ghost
Or prophecy
He does not ask
Fallen brother
The one who threw caution to horses
The needle in his arm
Leaving bloody tracks of equine poison
He was no equestrian
He was dirt under the hooves
His only bloodline
From the needle in his arm
He was not proud of his bloodline
This was not part of his Horse Nation
That which was his real legacy
The horse ran south

He saw a young man last night
With a gaping hungry mouth
A mouth that could only mouth the words
To sacred sounds
With no sound to emit from his inside
He studied the hunger in his face
In his eyes, the rough face
That peered over the singers
The drum, the women, and wondered
He studied the young man
Tough leather jacket
Street black boots
Touched him
Reached to him
With his mind

The young sister at the circle
Telling of her abuse at the hands of the older men
He saw her sigh

Letting out huge breaths of air
What was she saying?
He did not know. He did not ask
With watchful grace
She peered from safe vantage point
He once saw a wolf do the same thing
He recognized that look
Pure coat ruffling
Silently in the wind
Elusive from pursuers and companions alike
She is detached from the pack
Moving silently
Leaving the surge of her energy
Briefly with tall standing birch

No scrolls would tell of her passing
The birch would yield no clues
Her footprints disappearing in time
Becoming one with tracks of snowshoe hare, squirrel, and fox
Would she ever know the healing
Energy of tall standing birch
Peering with watchful grace?
He did not know. He did not ask

Sometimes the search was desperate
Other times, he couldn't give a damn
Sometimes the blues were as deep as the darkest blue could be
Other times, they were indigo
Or the colour of the sky
Still, other times, they were a fierce swirl of all hues
All hues of the colour blue
Sometimes lonely felt like a bone scraped clean
Chewed and spit out like powder
This reminds him of a story about an Aborigine in Australia
Who filled his mouth

With powder that came from the earth
And made colours; white and red
After filling his mouth
Placing his hands on the rocks
Or the hidden walls of caves
Spits the colours all over his hands
Leaving an outline on the rocks
Or on the hidden walls inside caves, forever
If he could do it
He would fill his mouth with the powdered bone
And spit the outline of his soul
Someone would come along
See a splash of blue alongside white and red
They would wonder who left
Imprints of powerful hands and blue soul
A blue whirlwind soul
Spit from the mouth of hollowed bone
The mouth
A sacred tool of earth paint
Blue bone mixed with spit and sky

The Phlebotomist

It was so easy
to stumble into your arms
from the streets of Franklin & Chicago
in 1979, in Minneapolis.

It was your job
to snap the rubber tourniquet tight
to pierce the vein
to watch my dark red blood
flow into the clear plastic bag
the blood rushing from my temple
from my heart.

Children of the Seventh Fire

We are the children
who wonder
if our fathers and mothers
will die drunk

We are the children
who heard promises of tomorrow
echoes of lies
like sounds from an empty drum

We are the children
who wake to nightmares
of tongues and cocks
between our legs
relatives brothers sisters
strangers smelling of piss
and wine in darkened rooms
unable to scream yell or tell
nightmares from nightmares
heaps of drunken humans
passed out on living room floors
fucking and groaning next to us

We are the children
with bloody faces
mothers and sisters
in ransacked houses
police lights flashing

We are the children
who walk through glass
without flinching
tattoo scars cigarette burns

razor cuts on arms legs and bodies
tell our self-mutilation

We are the children
who grit our teeth

We are the children
of stolen dreams
hearts pierced
by sharpened crosses
of vampires
in frocks and white collars
and black habits
needing to exorcise themselves

We are the children
who will not let you sleep

We are the children
who became the abusers
wanting to stay warm
in the heart of fires
gone dead

We are the children
who learned that our bodies
weren't worth much
who believed love was sex
and sex was love
and if love felt so empty
why was it so important to be loved anyway

We are the children
who ran back home
to rapes gang bangs and blood

not believing women
are the earth

We are the children
who never heard the songs
believing our drums were hollow
taught to be silent
by threats and beatings
no one ever heard

We are the children
who hid in dark corners
starving
taught to fear the shadows
of ourselves

We are the children
wanting it to be gone
after saying it once
having to say it again and again

We are the children
who will name it
who will tear away the masks
and call it healing

We are the children
taught to survive
that's all.

A Braid is Like a Rosary

His hair is holy.
Each twist on the left
in memory of relatives passed on.
Each twist on the right
a prayer for the living.
Grey streaked braids hang long
last prayer at his waist
fingers on his last bead.
A braid is like a rosary
A rosary with roots.

In the Face of a Son

The memories that I've had lately
pertain to the sadness that I've seen in your face
since Lucy passed away.
Your oldest daughter, my oldest sister, my old dad.

I remember, in school, for father's day
the teacher would get us to make these cards—
made for somebody else's father.
You never smoked a pipe, had slippers
or read the paper in your easy chair.
You never wore a suit, much less a tie.

You weren't the father coming home
to greet your family after a hard day at the office.
There was no white picket fence, no fireplace
and no mom greeting you from the kitchen in full apron,
asking, "How was your day dear? Dinner will be ready in
half an hour."

So why did we all have to make these cards the same?
You sure weren't a white father, though you had short
trimmed hair.
The pipe holder I made for you in wood shop in high school
sat empty at your bedside, then made its way
to the kitchen, to the junk drawer,
and eventually disappeared altogether.

The things I remember now
help me to sort out the pain from the images of you
sawing wood, splitting it, and hauling it in.
I've had to learn to separate those memories of pain
from the knowing that I have today, of a hard-working man
busting his ass for white loggers to keep his family

from starving, and the look of a father
after losing two of his children—
one to a dangerous curve, the other to cancer.
It is that look that I see
when you think there is no one looking.

You weren't the tie, the pipe, the slippers, or the paper.
You were all of those other things and more.
I am looking. And now, I see.

There are moments of thinking that I could almost do it.
Almost muster enough courage to bring up those questions
I've wanted to ask, always wondered about—always.

For example, what did you think
about those little boy gestures of stepping up to you
putting something into your hand without looking at you,
without waiting to hear what you'd say?

I remember you asking me once, when you had been drinking,
"How come you never talk to me? I'm your son."
I wanted to laugh at your mistake but, instead, said
"I don't know." Then, closed the door.

Were we both afraid to speak to one another?
Somehow, I just can't imagine you being afraid of me.

With my oldest son, I have been glimpsing the reasons
behind your silence, my fear, and my uncertainty.
Watching and listening to myself
in the ways that I deal with the sometimes uncomfortable
moments between a father and his son.
How much is there. How much you are there.
How much you are here.
I am beginning to understand

the years of silence between us,
only because I can't bear
the moments of silence between my son and me.
It is true, then.
You do return, somehow, to those days
of being a little boy or a little girl,
catching glimpses of who you are,
where you came from, and why.
Where you came from, and why.
Except, I don't have to turn my head back.
I don't have to turn back.
It is here in the present,
in the future of my son's face, in his eyes,
and I see you.

On the Raspberry Trail

Yesterday
we picked raspberries
visited the river
twelve miles downstream
sat at the rapids and listened
my little girl
5 years old
listens as I talk
about selling blueberries as a kid
after picking all day in the muskegs
she asks me if I can teach them
the things I did
when I was small
her warm little hand touched me
like memory
as I answered yes
that's what we're doing
satisfied, she said, "I know"
I listen
as my youngest son
tells his siblings about the uncle
he has never met
but is named after
Graham Lee **Abraham** Hunter
I leap inside
at what to me is startling
heart-tugging revelations of history
as my youngest son explains why
his third name is Abraham
Questions follow;
How old was he when he died?
Was he your oldest brother?
Did you go to his funeral?

You were twelve years old when he died?

He was 25. Today, he'd be 46.
Yes. Yes. Yes.
He'd take me everywhere with him
he wouldn't that night

Did you used to live in Lorraine's house?
(It's the old family house)
Yes, there were 14 of us
Where did you all sleep?
We slept three to a bed
I slept between Abe and Bob
on an old bed
in the living room

Yesterday
we picked raspberries
visited the river
twelve miles downstream
sat at the rapids and listened
warm hands of memory
touching me
footsteps behind me
questions for the future
remembering
why I am here.

Boot

I wasn't there
the night the thread broke
the night you kicked away the chair
the night your esophagus meshed
with the veins in your neck

Sometimes I see you flying by
in a cherry red firebird
with big wheels
Sometimes I see you laughing—
never could see your eyes laughing
your glasses were too dark

Always with the remembering
I come back
to this vision of you
Your feet dancing
with unwilling partners
the chair already gone
Your hands tucked up
under the rope
meshed to your esophagus

Perhaps you wished to leave a light on
in the big picture window
for someone driving by

Water

Water is the blood of the earth. Water sustains all life. It is said that the amount of water that covers the earth's surface directly correlates to the amount of water that makes up the human body. We are the same. The earth is mostly water. We are mostly water. Water is the blood of the earth. Water sustains all life.

It is said that women are the keepers of water. The earth is a woman. We call her our mother. The respect we show women directly correlates to the respect we show the earth. The earth is a woman. The earth is our mother. The two are the same. Water is the blood of the earth. Water sustains all life.

Because these directly correlate, we need to consider what has happened within these contexts and what continues to happen all over this island we call our mother. They are one and the same. When we do this and look at how women are treated today and how they have been treated, particularly in the last 500 years, we see the direct correlation between these two dynamics. They are one and the same. In order to be part of the earth's healing we first must consider how we, as human beings, as men, as peoples, as societies contribute to what has happened to the earth—a woman. The two are one and the same. Water is the blood of the earth. Water sustains all life.

When plants are born, when trees are born, when flowers are born, they emerge from the womb of our mother—the earth. They become medicine. Nourished by water, the lifeblood of the earth, they emerge. When children are born, when little girls are born, when little boys are born, they emerge from the womb of the mother on a small river of water and blood and placenta. They become medicine. The two are one and the same. The treatment we show women, the treatment we show children, directly correlates to how we treat the earth, to how we treat the plants, the trees, the flowers, to how we treat our medicine. The two are one and the same. Water is the blood of the earth. Water sustains all life.

We need to pause and consider these things and directly correlate them to our own lives, directly correlate them to our own healing, directly correlate them to the healing of our families, directly correlate them to the healing of our communities, directly correlate them to the healing of our nations, directly correlate them to the healing we need to sustain within ourselves. We are medicine. Our children are medicine. Water is medicine. The trees are medicine. The earth is medicine. The earth is water. We are water. Water is the blood of the earth. Water sustains all life. Miigwitch!!

Dreams on a Horse

Yes. The Horse. I cannot tell you much, except to say that the Horse is holy. Perhaps that is not enough to say of it. The Horse is not unconnected with my life. There are things about the spiritual power of horses I do not understand. Yet. When I was younger I was always very much afraid of horses. There was something mysterious and powerful that made me look at them with fear and foreboding. At times I am still afraid of a Horse. No explainable reason really, it is just there. I was nearly kicked by a horse once when I was small. A very large draft horse, a very large, black, draft horse. One that everyone said was mean and unpredictable.

Horses were used to haul wood, hay and other such things. In summer they pulled a wagon. In winter they pulled a dray. The dray was handmade of log and timber, and was very heavy. I still remember Gilbert Blackbird driving those two big horses, one white, the other black. He seemed to know what to do with them when they got out of hand. I remember hearing more than one story about those horses getting away from him or taking off, running wildly through the snow, or through the fields if it was summer. I remember hearing about the time they got away from Old Joe Major. He was still on the dray, or the wagon, or whatever they were pulling at the time.

Maybe they just got tired of pulling those damn things around, people pulling at their mouths with metal bits, and the slap of leather on their backs. I remember seeing them once running down the road, an empty wagon reeling behind them and someone cursing at them from up on the hill. I remember hearing that the white one was female and the black one was male. I remember seeing my dad using those horses to haul wood; my dad looking so strong alongside those beautiful, scary, powerful animals. This is one of my most vivid memories. My dad alongside those horses, looking strong, beautiful, scary and powerful too. I suppose this has all had a lasting impression on me after all these years.

Yes. I still remember those big horses. The work horses as we called them. The mystery, the power and the beauty. The experience repeats itself again and again. What the mind is sees, and so repeats itself in words about those old memories of old men and old horses. I suppose that's the way life works. And now I see that there is much more to say.

Al Hunter

Manitou Rapids, Ontario

Al Hunter has published his poetry in many journals and anthologies, including *Poets Who Haven't Moved to Minneapolis, North Coast Review, New Breed,* and *Gatherings.* He is Anishinabe and a member of the Native Writer's Circle of the Americas and has performed his poetry in New Zealand, Canada, and the United States. Hunter co-chaired the committee which presented "Beyond Survival: The Waking Dreamer Ends the Silence," an international conference of indigenous writers and artists, in Ottawa, in 1993.

Denise Sweet

Eau Claire, Wisconsin

Prayer For Women Filled With Grace

Women who go hungry
delicately drink their tears
tipping hands like
lacy teacups to their mouths
whisper "All gone"
to themselves and
to their orphaned bodies;

Women going hungry
are eating themselves
not like Grandmother Spider
drawing a web from her body
spinning threads of glass
into death's timid puzzle,

but like a wolf gnawing to
free herself from steel jaws
women who go hungry are like wolves
hiding for days in their clothing
a burrow to warm their ivory bodies
lifting themselves in sacrifice
in a cult of suffering

To those women going hungry
whose porcelain faces are feverish
with blame,
whose voices mimic
the clear thin weeping of August rain:

Draw up like buckets from hollow wells!
Draw up like tin cups between prison bars!
The rich ooze of anger
will twirl around the tongue
while the eyes grow filmy with pleasure
it is this ritual of indulgence
that spoons and spills from within
the only appetite left to survive
this perfect hunger spell.

Water Poem

A small wood turtle staggers slowly
rocking to lift herself from the river
steadied she can still feel the pull
of the moon's blue rings; it's not
a simple act, resisting a river
both beautiful and dangerous
a river that pulls us in
with a logic of its own.

Today I stood remembering
this metaphor of persuasion
at the convergence of the
Wisconsin and the Eau Claire
I imagined the struggle: how
the body and the hardness of
reason would ride out
the blurry rebellion
toppling like twinbirds,
within a cage of bone.

Then while fishing, I waded through
weeds to retrieve Saxon's tangled line
branches lost to the thwack and swirl
of persuasive currents
float by like broken bodies
of shipwrecked suitors
I stand for a moment to regain balance
while small perch whirl around
my thighs like raw silk
and for that moment any fear
of dark water is forgotten.

the patternless weave and resistance
of this watery landscape conspires
a romance with drowning
but to stand or even swim

seems the secret to balance
between feverish shifts of twilight
that pull us in
and the rise of dark currents
that hold us in
we are at once disconnected and tethered
to this great gray mystery
while smooth stones dream of wings
beaks and gills gasp for air.

Evelyn Searching

Could I tell you how it is
to search the vacant faces
like lockers at a bus station,

to spend three days and two nights
waiting for the right time
to say father
or even sister?

Would it matter if I said
the looking and the finding
could split you in two
send you into empty caverns
of silence, fearful of the sound
of your own voice?

From White Earth to El Paso
the air grows thin and dry
Mexicans and Indians drift back
and forth between Juarez and El Paso
while the days dance red-hot through
the streets of old army barracks
turned neighborhoods:
This my father calls home.

My father is from Enemy Swim
where warriors baffled their enemies
by swimming the waters endlessly at night.
Here, the Rio Grande is a thin vein
transporting dust and deliverance
Here an enemy could walk across in silence.

Sister, I stand long and far from
any punishing storm of regret
and see in you how strangers
become fathers become strangers
in time and of choice.

And still we'll return—we always do—
as daughters or as mothers
lifting our children high above our heads
to change the color of the sky.

My Mother And I Had A Discussion One Day

and she said I was quite fortunate
to have two sons
and I said how is that? and she said
with daughters you worry for them
birth control, childrearing,
you worry for them, the threat of rape,
and then there is the wedding expense.
I looked into her tired eyes
and clouded face and saw
that she was quite serious.
Yes, but, I said,
boys eat more.

My mother and I had a discussion one day
and she said why do they call it
women's music?
and I said because they sing it,
take from it, feel good and strong
when they walk away from it
while we sit here this is going on.
Are you telling me, my mother said
up until now, I have been listening
and no women have been singing?
and I said that is right
and she said that was ridiculous
and hummed a tune
of her own.

My mother and I had a discussion one day
and she said why do you want to leave
this house, it is a fine house?
and I said I didn't think
there was much of a market
for a nosewiper, a kitchen keeper,
an under the bed sweeper
and she said my smart mouth
would get me in trouble one day
and I looked at her scarred knuckles
and quivering chin and realized

that I had spit in the face
of a thousand women and I wept
with my mother.

Fever Dreams

Through the open window
the trilling of crickets
like tiny clocks mark time
breaking the silence in my room.
I am weakened by an illness
I don't try to understand
I wait for the signs
I have learned to look for.
In a masquerade of fever-soaked sheets
I can hear myself talking in sleep
while my bed rises like an elevator
or like a plane shifting and wheeling
with the jet stream in my room
past piggy banks and coat hooks.

If I pay attention I can read the wattage
on the light bulb hanging dormant
from the cobwebbed ceiling
the dolls in the closet
shiver at the spectacle:
the rising and falling at will
the calliope of colors
the sight of me bouncing off
the walls and ceiling
spitting and sparking like a
distempered farm cat.

But it causes me no great concern
the drowsy laughter aboard a bed gone afloat
I've pulled up anchor and set sail
on a voyage of the sublime
like a beery-eyed sailor I call out
to my consorts in crime
the timid dollies huddle
in the closet clinging
to the Buster Browns.

It takes some convincing
but I descend to the island of sleep
later, a falling star will skid

over the tops of trees
and I will hear it
the wind will twirl sleep
like a luscious summer fan
into my eyes
the half-dressed dollies of the closet
will close their porcelain eyes
their breath coming so evenly in the darkness.

For Antone

Like a dangerous mural
on the walls of an underground transit
Antone dances across the gymnasium
of the correctional center
his long black hair
as though on fire
trails in its own inspired dance
his thin legs set in time
with the drum
"I used to dance fancy" he says
while the singer, an ex-offender
assesses the balance of stick against hide
the voice within the universe
grace within chaos.

The unit counselor observes
how Antone dances alone, this
common failure to engage
this low-impulse control
he makes notes on his staff chart
and calls in those
who have earned free time
Antone curses him, filing
into line with the others
they circle each other
like cautious wolves
it is a lonely round
and a dance they despise.

Within the chemdep unit
aboard a thin mattress, Antone
must dream to stay alive
he must imagine the smell
of maple syrup, the quiet conversations
over bowls of hot milk and bread
Auntie, pausing over black coffee
tries to remember how old the boy is now
they imagine each other

but cannot remember faces
since that time in Watersmeet,
when Antone danced fancy
and Auntie watched carefully
each time.

Mission At White Earth

1. While we walked around the cemetary
a crane flew over, a pterodactyl
against a sky filled with thunderheads
we read each marker, matched names
with names, until we come to "Tumahdee
infant son of . . ." Pennyroyal
has grown thick around the gravesite
and Phillip gently pulls away
the blue medicine of our relatives
until a proper clearing is made
once again.

2. Back then, Uncle Himhim tells us,
the catholics had a mission
here at White Earth, translating
gospels into Chippewa, routing
the children of all the villages
into their schools. At Christmas,
the children brought home memorized
verses from catechism class
and shared sacks of peppermint sticks
and cinnamon buttons with the oldtimers
slow to learn the English, he says and laughs.

3. At the Cass County Museum,
Phillip asks the volunteer behind the desk
about the bandolier bag displayed with photos
of White Earth Anishinabeeg; I point to
the glass case that holds property
of our families but she only works on Thursdays
and does not know about ownership
Phillip writes down a description of the bag
in his journal and whispers
"Let's get out of here."
The volunteer seems relieved
to tabulate our visit
in the museum guest book.

4. Before we leave White Earth, we return
to mission school, still
the tallest building here. Over here,
my mother points, we would butcher chickens
with Father McHenry, over there, a huge garden
she looks at the school in silence, at the boarded
windows, at the grounds grown over with neglect
Driving past the cemetary, Phillip recalls
the found grave marker of Tumahdee, my mother's brother
and upon return, we will plant again
the blue medicine of our relatives.

Here in America
for Pompeyo Lugo Mendez, Lac Courte Oreilles, November 1985

Here in America, he will say,
where wheat falls endlessly
beneath the cutter's blade
where women in summer dresses
stir their rich espresso
write poetry and compare affairs,
you are not afraid of ignorance,

Nor are you afraid to speak plainly
or to confront. In my country
young poets sing and have pistols
forced into their mouths
by the security forces. Those who live
bear a four-inch scar
so close to carotid
that any heart stops at the sight
of its fierceness.

When he says the word "political"
the sound is like the fast click
of stiletto heels on a city street.
He looks into his hands to find the words—
how can he show what he has seen?
It is a thin language, this English.

Like Neruda, he does not wish to please Them,
to sing their love songs, or to compose
clever lyrics about the homeland. He would
rather stumble forever in darkness
than pretend to marvel at the blaze
of burning buildings
or at the death of light itself.

While he sings of home, his eyes close
as if in a dream, in reverence—we cannot tell.
And when he plays his guitar at daybreak
he takes us to the place

where a mother is singing in Guarani
to her infant son Pompeyo
songs to awaken the Americans
from their long and murky slumber.

Losing to the Breakfast of Champions

I suppose I imagine it to be much worse
than it is: the flakes that are not flaky
the toasties that don't feel toasted
the wheat that boasts of germ and bran
is closer to shrewd than shred

It is not as though I regret the ritual
of adding the sugar, the fruit
the cream, the spoon
or the mantra of each yawning deliverance
to mouth from spoon to bowl
to spoon to mouth

Perhaps it is the voice of my mother
insisting that all of this be eaten
or the newsclipping on the refrigerator
anecdotes of spoiled children
the horrid breakfasts of sweet rolls
and hot chocolate

Or the hideous claims that cold pizza
and party punch contribute to street crime
or the rumor that sheila beddingheim
grew up to be quite promiscuous
because she ate no breakfast at all.

Winter Farm Auction

The pathway to their garden
has all but disappeared
onion sets like angry fists
have pushed themselves
through the frozen soil.

Pumpkin hearts have split
themselves in two
angry at being left behind
their vines
stiff and dry as snake skin
tangle in the molding leaves.

Stalks of corn lean together
like old women
pausing to mourn the scowl
of cold November winds.

Tilted seed caps block
the afternoon sun while eyes
follow the Homelite chainsaw
black and heavy, it goes for 25.

An Amish woman wears her cap recklessly
raising her number high for doilies
in a porcelain dishpan.

Somewhere a clang of horseshoes
and old garden tools are brought out
into the open like quarreling roosters
they are examined by the crowd of gamblers.

The auctioneer assembles the parcels
into a wooden crate and raises them up
high above the crowd, he asks
who will give him a dollar bill.

In September: Ode to Tomatoes

In September, the order of business
will always begin with tomatoes
the passionate fruit
of defiant grandmothers
of bachelor lords
in their kitchens of chaos
and of the occasional gardeners like myself
who can marvel the wonders of nature
while complaining of lower back pain.

Even then, the flaming Big Boys
and voluptuous Romas gather themselves
in dishpans, in aprons, yes, even at the doorstep
waiting for the enthusiasm of an early riser
to spill with poetic love
over a Mason or a Kerr of the stewed,
the brewed, the blended, the pureed:
this is destiny,
this is immortality,
this is salsa
in the dead of winter!

Tomatoes suspended in jars,
smiling their fetal smiles
outshining the corn relish
and the bony heaps of mutant squash
23 PINTS OF TOMATO MARMALADE
CANNOT HELP BUT PERSIST WITH THE IDEA OF SPRING
amidst the basement darkness
and the stacks of dying Milwaukee Journals.

Yes, even though we walk through valleys
of shadowy Death,
we will always can tomatoes
we will ladle together
the green into red
secrets into sauce
we can because we can
and not because we must.

Grace's Funeral

It's a dying shame that it's
always an adult who wallows in
serious error with such explanations
"Like sleeping but then it's not."
Children, emotional spot checkers
at funerals tug and pull for answers
asking the forgivable questions
wondering whether Grace can fly now.

At Auntie's house, the relatives
sit with plates of food on their laps
with plastic forks and no appetite
But the children are indeed hungry
for stories of the Dead People:
the neighbor who mistook his wife
for an outlaw and shot her
a simple case of mistaken identity.
This happens.

Or the boy who watched his twin brother
choke on a chickenbone and only the day before
had asked an adult about the Heimlich maneuver
or the aunt who never married but would often
sleepwalk and once off a bridge she fell
into the shallows holding the morning mail
most everyone certain she could not fly.

Wenebozho in Cream City

when the sun rises, he will be there
remaining after he is asked
to leave; he does not hear this
or this: "No, you can't"
"It has never been done"
he laughs and never sleeps
and asks with a voice
like a canyon
"Will you write poems about me?"

And then suddenly he is warm emerald water
a tide coming this close to your feet
and then skittering away
a champion of concealment
an illusion of the landscape
— it has never been easy for me
a whisper that drains like ground glass
from memory,
or like a child twisting gently
from your hand,
gone before you know it.

Constellations

. . . They had to name, they had to remember,
or things would not be named and remembered
if they did not do it.   — Carlos Fuentes

These are the new stories,
our response
to the sorrow
of light arriving
and dying
the stellar maps of
story and myth
where writers find
their way back
to beginnings
riding like black
satin horses
charging
the silvery landscape.

This is to remember

Our wounded and
dead. This is to remember
the names
we've given away
or never received.

This is to love the forgotten.

To Know By Heart: Saulte St. Marie, October 1989
for Conrad

I. In Batchawana Bay, a slight womanrain
    casts a pewter haze while houses disappear
    in shadows of the mountainous strata
    pale pink ribbons of lights glide
    slowly over the horizon. Here you need no maps,

    One finds the way by heart, you say. While
    Pre-cambrian shields bear the scars of our absence
    stories of how Anishinabe blood shored into stones,
    of how the old man returned them to soft graves
    We were here. We're still here. This place.

II. The colors are different at Blind River, you say
    there, your map is the canvas, your colors
    the reflection of flint upon water and ridge
    your unusual recall—a palette for heartbreak.

    When you run to the petroglyphs, you leave behind
    the poison of frustration—like the paintings
    of the bushmen, the wind whirls away scorpion patterns
    above your head, beneath your heart until the heart
    can rise high above any pain of history
    any pain of remembering.

III. We step into the trading post while a black dog removes
    himself slowly from the entrance. He is tolerant
    of the tourists and has grown sadly arthritic, this one
    who could sleep for nights under a sky of ice and stars.
    He belongs here and we do not.

    We wander alone through aisles of mass production
    of miniature canoes and other half-priced authenticities
    until we fall silent at the sight of insane opulence:
    a foxskin tossed amidst a display of carved pipes and katchinas

    I felt stupid and shy about tears I could not show you

When you explained how the templehairs of moose are dyed
and trimmed close into the shapes of flowerbuds. Before
leaving, you hand me a gift—a small carved bear.
Makwa, my dodem rises, swelling with the warmth of wood,
and the fenugreek odor of hands carving away the difference.

"Makwa" is the Ojibwe term for "bear"; "dodem" is loosely
translated to refer to a totemic ancestor.

Zen and Woman's Way of Parking

We know sooner than we think
when the vehicle we are driving
refuses to be herded into its stall.
We crank the wheel and ease our way
around and in and back and forth
and then back out and forward and in
again and then back and forth and
back and forth 'til we have neatly
and carefully negotiated a big thing
into a small space. "It's all in the
wrist" when we speak of power steering
or, for that matter, our lover. And yet,

it is a maneuver that requires integration
of our body, mind, and spirit. The contortive
efforts of the driver imitate Hatha yoga
positionings, as we are expected to see
front and behind, this side and that side
All at the same time. Be in the here and now
in the parking lot. Serenity is not far behind.
Neither is the Volvo parked in the next lane.

And how quickly we computate space, density,
width, length and probability at that moment we
grind the gears from first to reverse and back
again; after careful deliberation, the geniuses
that we are, we arrive at the parking nudge
principle: simply put, it is necessary and
a tender act to nudge the vehicle to the front
and back of us as we locate parameters of the
space we are to become. Oh to be parked in a
stall of our own, but spiritually connected with
all that exists around us. Nirvana is achieved.

And the headlights are on.

Let them call us "ladydrivers" let them curse
and shake their fists at "the battle axe behind
the wheel." We'll give them no fast break,
no free ride; indeed we will not yield

even though the sign insists. Oh sisters,
this is the right of way revolution,
a woman's way of parking is knowing and seeing
and feeling our way around this hard, flat
landscape we call parking space. We have finally
come to a place of which we surely belong.
We are at last in the driver's seat,
and we laugh in the face of cruise control.

Night of Diamonds: January, 1993

Buried within winter slumber's smooth abandon
creeping rhythms of sleep's silent cadence
comes in single beats. Again. Again.
We draw our fasting breath while
prismed lights are drumming
the horizon; the ground
beneath borrows the
warmth of women
gathering for
renewal

Some
where sits
a wolf pulling in
the raw and frozen air, and
somewhere it is about to snow again.

the Longhouse floor worn hard and bare from
dancing creaks and snaps as woodstoves
warm and the logs are bedded among
embers glimmering like diamonds
the little ones climb the
benches to smear the
window with a kiss
frost feathers
form from
breath

as a
young girl
slowly recounts
the address of gratitude
standing shyly with her back
to her female relatives who are
gathered in a circle surrounding all
the ancestors have come here to listen
and to warm their bones from the fire among us
even the sweet moon spills light in delight while some
where sits a wolf pulling in the raw and frozen air, and somewhere

it
is about
to snow again.

Sensible Shoes

It is not their comfort
that turns me away
or their simple line,
strict defining way about them
or that they gently bend my arch
to meet a contour proper,
or even the tiptoe quiet
as I enter the room
unnoticed by other shy and quiet soles.

I turn away from the safe
and sensible shoe, the saddle
or the loafer,
harbour a foolish longing
for the pump or the spike
Even now I lay awake at night,
imagining the sore but earned
achilles tendon, dreaming
my flat feet lifting me to reach
another's lips, tiny feet with pointed toes
perhaps a low slung strap or
seductive heels in whorish red velvet.

How odd to covet the bound foot, the
treacherous tottering in black patent
stilettos, toes that numb and stiffen
in the unwieldy glass slipper
The dread I will never dance with others
in my sensible shoes, size seven and a half
slightly worn at the toe and heel.

A Fear of Dark Places
with love to Aunt Julia

Sometimes you have cried so long, there is little left to do but be still. You are lucky this way; there is no risk in listening to your own heartbeat. You have only wandered too far and the only way back is to stay where you are. What do you think of now? How it is to be forgotten? To be remembered as lost? An old stone woman throws open her window and beckons you to move closer to the ledge. She tells you that there is warmth near her fire. You begin to crave the details of the story she tells; the warm bread she has baked, the red willow tea she has sweetened for you with the syrup from her trees. Your fear of dark places has made you squirm so closely to the fire that you cannot resist the flames. Even the shadows claim the pleasure of your own safety. The halo of the fire seems so pure to you that you have lost your feeling for pain. Do not risk this, even if darkness becomes your only ally. The Owl can be a comfort to you now. His heart is as still as the moonlight as he waits for the muted animal, far from the house of tremble, far from the stone woman. Be quiet and listen. Few of us can understand how darkness helps us to stay alive. Even birds move away from us in fear.

2 AM Memory
for Sharon Olds

What awakens at 2 am
is not the two lovers
quarrelling
outside your window
weaving their way
towards an awkward bed

Nor the thin and spindly
sound of crickets
or the blister of twilight
rising over the sill.

Bad poetry.

What awakens at 2 am
is my argument with memory
tough and hard
like peachstones
too large and bitter
for eating.

At 2 am is the seed
of remember
so full and gorgeous
and hard to negotiate
let alone
swallow.

The Religion of Stones

Without thinking, we drop two stones
perilously into the precipice
one, courageous in its descent
fires the path with shrill light
it goes beyond aloneness
unbodied, beyond the unnamed
to fall away from reluctance
in concentric circles
pooling its inevitable
waves back to us.

The other arcs with
the velocity of confusion
veers and tangles with
the memory of ascent
like fever dreams
the other shudders and flees
moves through wind and rain
while a quiver of small wings
appears, then suddenly
its pewter body, blood warm
silhouettes against
the white crest of clouds.

There is a reason for everything, he said.

Still Born
for Toni

Pearl-white, we bathed you
cocooned in soft flannel folds
and delivered you like an effigy
to the nurse, her head shook once as
she touched your chest, your starfish hands,
your tiny head, elongated and wet with anguish.

The coolant in the room begins to hiss
(you would've shivered and cried for home—
there, a bassinet gauzed in ivory lace
and a rocking chair wait, heaped with gifts—
one, a t-shirt that reads, "Spoiled Rotten")

But, what did it feel like, the burden
of mottled birth unto cold, wet sheets?
Ghost-like and timid, what did you feel?
The paralysis of silence, cold steel
against your spine, your body caging
tiny murmurs of warmth, a stubborn secret?

As the spasms boil within an amniotic river
a gray-green mueconium swaddles you
your tiny neck, swollen and collared,
drops the weight gladly into gloved hands
reluctance is your only grace
your birth, an empty still relief.

Your sparrow heart collapsed into dark ponds
of blood: Lovely pearl, did you feel her
legs quiver around you, their hands struggle
to resurrect you? Did you hear the sputter
of the aspirator? Or the sharp ping of
the surgical knife as it hit the floor?

Would you have carried us, let us reconcile
the seconds of your life into years just once?
We would press these lips against your chest
till the heart tones leapt across the screen
like silvery sprites—instead a harsh, blank,
lunatic silence levels the walls around us.

Dancing the Rice

The fall season enters the rhythms of our pace
leaves gather like whorls on a spindle of wind
twisting and coiling around our feet;

the old man sits in front of the fire stirring
and singing low in whispers to himself, tossing
the rice slowly in the bottom of the black pot;

the good grain, manomin, turns slowly from green
to darkened fibers in the heat, we watch it turn
small swirls of steam wisp away from the parching;

the helper, a young man, slowly slips into moccasins
recalls that they belonged to his grandmother, and once
were too small for his feet—but they grew with him;

when we dance, he says, we caress the earth
we carry power in the way we present ourselves
as dancers, as singers, bringing the rice home;

this power enters each stem of manomin
but it must be a gentle step, the padding of feet
against the good grain; they hold our dreams

and we must be slow and gentle when we dance the rice
or they can quickly turn to broken stems and then to dust
then we have nothing and the manomin will not return.

He lowers himself into the barrel of parched rice
placing his feet gently against the heated grain
slowly lifting one foot, and twisting the other

he shifts his hips side to side; hoisting his weight
on the sides of the barrel, he gently kneads the grain
pressing each step in a circle against the barrel's bottom

"Everything tries to go in a circle. Everything in nature.
You and me. Yuh." The old man watches while the rice is tossed
from the basket into the air—tiny whirlwinds of chaff spring

forth like dervishes released from a magic lamp. The wind
sails them away from the winnowed rice—the grain chinks against
the birchbark basket in cadence with the dropping wrists and

the young man's swaying black hair—it is a dance of sweet and
gentle love—warming hearts and pleasing the old man who watches
and sees in circles, our survival embodied in the winds of October.

Denise Sweet

Eau Claire, Wisconsin

Denise Sweet is an assistant professor at the University of Wisconsin–Green Bay, currently teaching poetry, fiction, and American Indian literature. Her work has appeared in *Calyx, Upriver, The Best of NOTA, Plainswoman, Political Palate, Sinister Wisdom, Transactions, Wisconsin Poetry, Bearing Witness: An Anthology of Native American and Chicano Women's Writing,* and *Women Brave in the Face of Danger.* Her first collection of poems, entitled *Know by Heart* (Rhiannon Press) was published in 1992. She recently received the Outstanding Indian Woman Award from the Positive Indian Development Center and the Wisconsin Women's Council. She is Anishinabe, enrolled at White Earth, a Minnesota Ojibwe reservation.

Jim Northrup

Sawyer, Minnesota

Rez to JEP to Rez

The birch and popple leaves were yellow. The red of the maple had come and gone. It was warm in the afternoons.

Luke Warmwater and his wife for life, Panequay, were making rice in the back yard. Their part of the season's gift had been harvested and parched. She was dancing and he was fanning.

As they worked, they watched the occasional car going by the house. They talked about the people that went by. The cars they didn't recognize were automatically classified as tourists. A familiar car went by.

"That's your cousin, isn't it?" she said.

"Yup."

"How are you related to him?" she asked.

"Let's see now." Luke paused in his fanning. He resumed fanning and said, "His dad and my grandma on my dad's side were brother and sister."

"Your cousin huh?"

"Yup, my cousin."

Panequay enjoyed the shish-shish sound the rice made as she danced. Luke looked closely at his fanning basket. He was thinking how it could be made better next year. Luke liked the color of the translucent green rice. It made a rhythmic sound as it bounced in the basket. The empty hulls drifted with the wind.

A customized van pulled into the driveway. They didn't recognize it until the driver got out.

"Looks like Dave has got himself a California van."

"I wonder what he wants, he usually doesn't visit us."

"I guess we'll find out, here he comes."

Dave walked over to where they were working. He said hello to both of them. Dave settled into a lawn chair and said, "Who'd you learn that from—making rice?"

"From everyone I ever watched," answered Luke.

"My grandmother used to make rice like that."

"Not many people do it this way anymore."

"It's so much easier to do it with machines."

"I think hand-finished rice tastes better," said Luke.

"It cooks easier too," added Panequay.

They were about done making rice for the day. She covered the pit she was using. Luke gathered up the baskets and rice. He carried the rice and baskets inside. The hand cleaning could be done as they watched TV. Luke invited Dave in for coffee.

They sat down in the living room and drank coffee. Dave talked about paddy rice. "That paddy rice sucks, my wife cooked some for an hour and a half and it still wasn't tender."

"I've heard it called driveway rice," laughed Luke.

"Driveway rice?"

"Yah, when you get stuck in your driveway, you throw that stuff under the wheels for traction."

"That's about all it's good for," said Panequay.

Luke rewound the tape on the VCR as they talked.

"Want to watch JEP with us?" asked Luke.

"Sure, I like JEOPARDY!" he said.

Watching JEOPARDY! was a family tradish with the Warmwaters. They liked to match wits with the Chimooks on the tube.

Luke was having a good day—snapping out the questions before the contestants. Dave was mentally keeping track of Luke's winnings. On Double and Final JEOPARDY! Luke always yelled, "All of it."

When Final JEOPARDY! was over, Luke was $13,000 ahead of the players on the program. He always bet the entire amount because this was only TV.

"Do you always do that?" asked Dave.

"Make rice? Sure, every year," answered Luke.

"No, I mean play JEOPARDY! like that?"

"We usually watch it live, unless we're doing something, then the VCR watches it for us."

"Do you always win like that?"

"Oh sure, for a compulsive reader it's easy," bragged Luke.

Dave thanked them for the coffee and left. A plan was forming as he walked out to his van. Luke and Panequay continued cleaning their rice.

Dave came to the Warmwater house again the next day. He said he wanted to learn how to make rice. Luke let him do some fanning. When he spilled some on the ground, Luke suggested he should also learn how to clean rice. He sat him down where there wasn't a chance of spilling any more rice.

Once again they went inside to drink coffee and watch JEP with the VCR. Luke was having an even better day snapping out questions. Dave took out a small calculator and kept track of Luke's earnings. When Luke doubled his winnings on the Final JEOPARDY! question, Dave proposed a deal. "If I pay the costs out there and back—make all the arrangements—would you split half and half, you know, 50-50?"

"Maybe," said Luke in a noncommittal monotone.

"Yesterday I called Merv Griffin Enterprises. I got an appointment for you to take the test—a preliminary screening."

"Where is 'out there'?"

"Hollywood, we have to go to Hollywood. We can go in my van, take turns driving."

"I'll let you know tomorrow," said Luke.

After Dave left, Luke and Panequay talked about going to California. They were almost done making rice, so they had the time.

"Why not, it'll make a nice break."

"I haven't been out there in quite a while," she said.

Luke called Dave and told him they were ready to leave for California. Dave came to their house. Luke threw their clothes and a cribbage board in the van. They left the rez.

The freeway was boring through Iowa and Nebraska. Luke and Panequay played cribbage in the back of the van. Long rolling hills, each crest was about five miles from the last one. Luke kept expecting to see something different at each crest. He didn't—each crest looked the same as the last. The freeway looked the same all the way to the mountains.

The mountains were more interesting. They gradually climbed through Colorado. Near Aspen, they saw about 40 miles of condominiums. They looked at the mining scars on the sides of the steep mountains. The weather in the mountains was about a month ahead of the weather back home on the Fond du Lac Reservation.

Luke looked at the green lodgepole pine and yellow quaking aspen. The freeway followed every curve of the Colorado River. They reached 10,000 feet before they started to go downhill. Luke knew it was downhill because he began to see runaway truck ramps. Some of them were used recently.

At one point, the freeway, the river and the mountains came real close together. Luke said, "Boy, that white guy can build a road anywhere, can't he?"

The Rocky Mountains continued to amaze the flatland Indians. At one spectacular view, Luke was moved to say, "Way to go, God."

He wondered where that expression came from, then he remembered. It was from a Ziggy cartoon. The view kept changing as they continued west. It got to the point where they abbreviated it.

"Look over there, there's another W.T.G.G."

"Yup, way to go, God."

Luke and Dave had both driven and were tired. It was Panequay's turn. Dave crawled in the back and Luke fell asleep in the front seat.

He woke up when there was a particularly loud crash of thunder. The van was swaying around the corners on the rain-slick mountain road. The windshield wipers were working erratically.

Panequay was drinking coffee, snapping her gum loud and smoking a cigarette. She was hunched over, her knuckles were white where they bent around the wheel.

"Maybe if you slowed down a bit, it wouldn't be as scary," Luke told his wife.

She slowed down and began to relax as she drove down the mountain into the deserts of Utah and Arizona.

Luke and Panequay started talking about Las Vegas right after they crossed the Nevada state line. Dave must have overheard them because he sat up and said, "I've got another plan—let's spend the night in Las Vegas. We can get up early and still be on time for your test."

"Is this the reason we came this way?" said Luke, remembering the stories of Dave and his love of gambling.

"Could be," confessed Dave.

He then told them of the many times he had won many thousands of dollars gambling in Las Vegas.

Luke and Panequay got a motel room. Dave didn't need one because he was going to gamble all night. After they showered and changed, they went out to eat.

They were walking back to the motel when they decided to try their luck in a casino. The two Indians sampled all the games of chance. After Keno, video poker, slots and roulette, they decided they liked the blackjack tables the best.

Luke quickly spent his gambling allowance. Panequay was doing good on the tables. They left the casino when she was a couple of hundred dollars ahead.

The next morning they checked out and waited by the van to meet Dave. Luke saw Dave swaggering down the street.

"How'd you do?" Luke asked.

"I got $4,700 here," he said as he pulled out a wad of greenbacks. All the bills in the wad looked like fifties.

"Good, let's go then—I've got to take a test and then get back home and finish making rice," said Luke.

"You drive then, I've got to get some sleep," said Dave, crawling in the back of the van.

Luke drove from Las Vegas through the Mojave Desert. As they passed over a bridge, Luke asked Panequay, "Do you know why the fish in the Mojave River wear goggles?"

"No, why do they wear goggles?"

"To keep the sand out of their eyes," said Luke, pointing with his lips at the dry riverbed.

When they came down the mountains near San Bernadino, they saw a layer of something in the air.

"Is that fog?" she asked.

"No, I think it's smog."

"Remember what the air is like back home?" she asked.

"Yup, try not to breathe while we're in Los Angeles," he advised.

They wandered the freeways for a while. Eventually they found the off ramp they were looking for. Eventually they found the TV station where the JEOPARDY! test was administered. Luke had allowed plenty of dumb time to find the place. The dumb time was used up by the time they found a parking place.

Luke got out and waited by the studio gate. A line began to form behind him. There were about 60 people in line. He was the only one who wasn't white, the only Indian.

A contest coordinator came out and took charge.

"Welcome to the preliminary screening for JEOPARDY! contestants," he California-smiled as he addressed the hopeful. Luke could tell he had done this many times before.

The coordinator ushered them into the actual soundstage used for the JEOPARDY! program. Luke was slightly disappointed to see that Alex Trebek wasn't there.

The soundstage looked familiar, then Luke remembered that he had seen it about 250 times on his TV back home. He noted the APPLAUSE sign for the studio audience. Off to one side of the set was a director's chair. The red chair was labeled 'Alex Trebek.' Well, at least I get to see where he parks his ass between takes, Luke thought.

The coordinator passed out answer sheets and warned the hopeful that this was a difficult test. The hopeful watched a prerecorded tape. The questions came at ten-second intervals. There were 50 questions in 50 categories. Luke made a mark for each question he wasn't sure of. After the last question, the answer sheets were gathered up. They watched a JEOPARDY! tape while the tests were being graded. The 60 hopeful were yelling out questions at the TV set.

The contest coordinator came back and called six names. He thanked the 54 hopeless for their time and effort. The losers trooped out of the building, including Luke.

Panequay and Dave were waiting when Luke walked out. She could tell what had happened by looking at Luke's eyes.

"Well, how'd it go?" asked Dave.

"Half of nothing is nothing," answered Luke. "I wish they would have asked me questions I knew. There were nine out of fifty I missed. They don't tell you your score," continued Luke.

"What happens now?" asked Dave.

"Nothing, unless you want to try this trip again."

"I don't think so, I want to go to Las Vegas," said a disappointed Dave.

"What's the rush, enjoy the money you got now. We could play tourist here in Hollywood."

"No, I'm going to double my money when I get there."

When they got to Las Vegas, Luke got a motel room again. Dave rushed off after arranging a meeting place for the next morning. He had a gambler's gleam in his eye as he walked fast to the nearest casino.

Panequay gambled at the blackjack tables again. She was winning slowly but steadily. When she noticed a losing streak, she changed tables. Luke gambled big at the roulette and blackjack tables. He ran out of money real quick. He stood around and watched his wife win. She was over $500 ahead when she quit.

They went to another casino that was offering a prime rib dinner for $2.99. Luke played Keno while they were eating. He was using money he borrowed from Panequay. He didn't win.

The next morning they found Dave waiting outside the motel. He looked sad. His pockets were turned inside out. Luke could tell he hadn't won.

"Well, how'd it go?" asked Luke, being polite.

"I was $10,000 ahead," mumbled Dave.

"Was? Did you spend it all?"

"All of it, I was trying to stay up with the high rollers."

"Gas money too?" asked Luke.

"All of it, I don't know how we're getting home. I called a couple of people to send money but it doesn't sound too hopeful," explained a chastened Dave.

"How are you going to get us home?" asked Luke.

"I don't know," he told the sidewalk.

Luke didn't tell him about Panequay's luck at the blackjack table. After all, it was Dave's responsibility to get them to JEOPARDY! and back.

Dave went to a pay phone and tried calling his wife. She wouldn't accept his collect call. He slammed the phone down.

He talked about pawning his van. He said he would buy the Warmwaters bus tickets home.

"Wonderful, blow into town with a $2,000 van and leave town in a $40,000 bus," said Luke.

After he pawned his van, Dave planned on winning enough to get his van out of hock. He planned on winning enough for gas money, he planned on winning enough for food. He planned on winning enough to buy Las Vegas presents for his wife and kids.

When he checked, he realized he didn't have the title for the van. He couldn't hock the truck.

"I've got $50 she won. Do you want to eat or go back in and win what you lost?" asked Luke.

"I'll take that fifty and turn it into a couple of thousand," bragged Dave. He took the money and dashed into the nearest casino. Luke and Panequay waited outside.

Dave came out after a few minutes. He was walking slow.

"All of it?" asked Dave.

"All of it, they cleaned me out again. I can't believe it."

"Well, how do we get home now?" asked Luke.

"I don't know, I'll try calling my wife again," Dave told the sidewalk.

She wouldn't accept his call. He slammed the phone down. He went looking for his friend who worked at a casino. He couldn't find him, no answer on his phone either.

Dave checked at the Western Union to see if any of his previous pleas had been answered. They hadn't.

Finally when Dave started talking about robbing one of the high rolling winners, Luke told him that Panequay had enough money to get home. They left Las Vegas.

The trip home was grim. Dave was angry because they hadn't told him about the money. The Warmwaters were upset with Dave because he didn't pay their way home as promised. Luke and Panequay played cribbage through four states.

The Warmwaters bailed out when the van got to Minneapolis. They went to Luke's sister and asked for a ride home. She fed them and laughed at their Las Vegas story.

When they got home, they began to make rice again. Another yearly cycle was ending and beginning. The birch and popple leaves were now on the ground.

"We've got about four batches left to finish," said Luke.

"Is the VCR watching JEP for us?"

"Yup, we can clean rice while we watch it."

"I'm glad to be home," she said. She eye-thanked him.

"Are we going to stop in Las Vegas next time?"

"Next time, when are we going out there again?" she asked.

"I made another appointment in January for JEOPARDY!" he laughed. "This time we're not going with Dave."

Riding the Dog

It's been years since I rode the dog, the Greyhound. It was the usual wintertime dead car story. Car is broke and in the shop. My relatives that could have taken me were either at work or their cars were not working. I had to get to the Cities.

My sister dropped me off at the ticket agent in Cloquet on her way to work. I waved goodbye and went in and paid $18.00 for the one-way trip. I browsed the magazines while waiting for the 12:40 bus.

The big gray, silver, black and blue bus pulled in. The uniformed driver got out and told the waiting crowd that the bus was full. It was standing room only until Hinckley where two seats would be available. The only other alternative was to wait six hours for the next bus.

I had to get to the Cities. I got on the bus first because I knew the bathroom was in the rear. I really had to go.

I used the bathroom and joined the others who were standing in the aisle. They were hanging on to the seats and overhead racks as the bus swayed around the corners out of town. I stood there. The whole idea sounded silly. Stand up all the way to the Cities?

I knew there was an empty seat—the bathroom. I closed the lid on the blue water tank and sat down. It didn't smell like a bathroom in there. The seat was hard plastic but it would be easier than standing and swaying for three hours.

Using my briefcase, I propped the door open to show my fellow passengers that I was a social animal. The nearest ones laughed when they saw how I had solved my problem of standing all the way to the Cities.

I looked around my private sitting room. It was mostly glass and stainless steel. The main window was frosted glass and I couldn't see anything but light and shadows. There was a small plastic window that I could open so I could get fresh air. I propped the window open so I could enjoy the scenery of northern Minnesota. I couldn't see much besides snowbanks but did feel like I could control part of my environment.

The vibrations from the bus motor and transmission travel just fine through the plastic seat. I was almost beginning to enjoy the vibrations. My butt was getting numb after 60 miles so I stood for a while.

I entertained myself by reading the signs posted in my private sitting room:

> Lavatory has no water
> Do not drink this water please
> Please use wet naps to clean hands
> Door must be locked when using lavatory
> Please do not deposit hand towels in the toilet
> Use waste paper disposal located under counter
> Lock door to turn on light
> Emergency Exit
> Lift this bar and push window out

After I read all the signs I pulled some reading material out of my briefcase. I realized that I had more room than if I were sitting in one of the regular seats. I was able to open my newspaper full-width. I looked out and the other 47 passengers were sitting shoulder-to-shoulder. Four people still stood in the aisles. They looked like silent tour guides swaying there.

Greyhound bus #5056 roared on down Interstate 35. The vibrations were still pleasant. I thought of those motel vibrating beds.

When I finished the paper I was a little sleepy. I was able to drape myself over the sink while I took a little power nap.

After the smoke break at Grand Casino in Hinckley, the other passengers came back to use the bathroom. My private sitting room was not so private anymore. As they were coming up and down the aisle, I could see the strangers butt-rubbing as they squeezed by each other. After each one left I opened the window to air the place out.

I was glad when the bus driver announced the next stop was St. Paul.

The ride to the Cities in the bathroom wasn't too bad. The vibrating seat goes the same place the cushioned seats go. The ride was more Spartan but we all got to the Cities at the same time. It could have been worse. What if I had to stand up in the bathroom all the way to the Cities?

Once I got off the bus I never looked back.

Veterans Dance

Don't sweat the small shit, Lug thought, and it's all small shit unless they're shooting at you.

The tall skinny Shinnob finished changing the tire on his car. It took longer than usual because he had to improvise with the jack. Summer in Minnesota and Lug was on his way to a powwow.

The powwow was on its second day. The dancers were getting ready for their third grand entry. Singers around the various drums had found their rhythm. Old bones were loosening up. The M.C. was entertaining the crowd with jokes. Some of the jokes brought laughs and others brought groans. Kids were weaving through the people that circled the dance arena. The drum sound knitted the people together.

Lug brushed his long hair away from his face as he looked in the sky for eagles. He had been away from home a long time and was looking forward to seeing his friends and relatives again.

He really enjoyed powwows although he didn't dance. Lug was content to be with his people again. Ever since the war he felt disconnected from the things that made people happy.

The first time Lug walked around the arena he just concentrated on the faces. He was looking for family. While walking along he grazed at the food stands. He smelled then sampled the fry bread, moose meat and wild rice soup.

The Shinnobs walking around the dance arena looked like a river that was going in two directions. Groups of people would stop and talk. Lug smiled at the laughing circles of Shinnobs. He looked at faces and eyes.

That little one there, she looked like his sister Judy did when she was at that age. Lug wondered if he would see her at this powwow. Judy was a jingle dress dancer and should be at this powwow. After all, she only lived a mile from the powwow grounds.

The guy walking in front of him looked like his cousin that went to Vietnam. Nope, couldn't be him. Lug had heard that he died in a car accident last fall.

Sitting in a red and white striped powwow chair was an old lady that looked like his grandma. She wore heavy brown stockings that were held up with a big round knot at the knees. She chewed Copenhagen and spit the juice in a coffee can just like his gram. Of course, Lug's grandmother had been dead for ten years but it was still a good feeling to see someone who looked like her.

Lug recognized the woman walking toward him. She was his old used-to-be. He hoped she didn't want to talk about what went wrong with them. She didn't, she just snapped her eyes and looked away. Lug knew it was his fault he couldn't feel close to anyone. His face was a wooden mask as they passed each other. He could feel her looking at him out of the corner of her eyes. Maybe, he thought, just maybe.

He stopped at a food stand that was called Stand Here. Lug had black coffee and a bag of mini-donuts. The sugar and cinnamon coating stuck to his fingers when he finished. He brushed off his hands and lit a smoke. Lug watched the snaggers 8 to 68 cruising through the river of Shinnobs.

That jingle dress dancer looked like Judy, yup, it was her. The maroon dress made a tinkling, jingling sound as she came closer. She looks healthy, Lug thought. A few grey hairs but she moves like she was 20 years younger. They both smiled just as hard as their eyes met. Warm brown eyes reached out for the wary ones.

She noticed the laugh lines were deeper. The lines fanned out from the edges of his eyes. He looked like he had lost some weight since the last time she saw him. His blue jean jacket was just hanging on him, she thought.

Lug and Judy shook hands and hugged. Her black velvet bag hit him on the back as they hugged. They were together again after a long time apart. Both leaned back to get a better look at each other.

"C'mon over to the house when they break for supper," she said.

"Got any cornbread?" he asked.

"I can whip some up for you," she promised.

"Sounds good."

Eating cornbread was a reminder of when they were young together. Sometimes it was the only thing to eat in the house. Cornbread was the first thing she made them when he came back from Vietnam.

"I have to get in line for grand entry so I'll see you later. I want to talk to you about something," she said.

"Okay, dance a round for me."

"I will, like I always do."

Lug watched the grand entry. He saw several relatives in their dance outfits. He nodded to other relatives who were standing around the dance arena. Lug sipped hot coffee as the grand entry song was sung. He saw Judy come dancing by. He turned and looked toward his car.

He walked to his car as the flag song started. He almost moved in time to the beat as he walked. Lug was going to get his tire fixed at the truck stop. He closed the car door as the veterans' song came over the public address system.

Lug left the powwow grounds and slipped a tape in his cassette player. The Animals singing "Sky Pilot" filled the car. Lug sang and tapped his fingers on the steering wheel in time to the vintage music.

He drove to the truck stop and read the newspaper while the mechanic fixed his tire. Lug put the tire in the trunk, paid the guy and drove to his sister's house. He listened to the Righteous Brothers do "Soul and Inspiration" on the way.

Judy's car was in the driveway so he knew she was home. He parked, got out of the car and walked up to the front door. Lug rang the doorbell and walked in. He smelled cornbread.

She was in the kitchen making a pot of coffee. He sat at the kitchen table as she took the cornbread out of the oven. The steaming yellow bread made his mouth moist. Judy poured him a cup and sat down next to him.

"Well, how have you been?" she asked.

"Okay, my health is okay," he replied.

"Where have you been? I haven't heard from you in a long time."

"Oh, you know, just traveling here and there. I'd work a little bit and move on. For a while there, I was looking for guys I knew from the war."

"Where was that you called from last March?" she asked.

"D.C., I was in Washington D.C. I went to the Wall and after being there I had to talk to someone I knew."

"You did sound troubled about something."

"I found a friend's name on the Wall. He died after I left Vietnam. I felt like killing myself."

"I'm glad you didn't."

"Me too, we wouldn't be having this conversation if I had gone through with it."

She got up and cut the cornbread and brought it to the table. He buttered a piece and began taking bites from the hot bread. She refilled his cup.

"Remember when we used to haul water when we were kids? I was just thinking about that the other day. That one time when it was thirty below and the cream cans fell off the sled? You somehow convinced me it was my fault. I had to pump the water to fill the cream cans again. You told me it was so I'd stay warm. I guess in your way you were looking out for me," she said.

"Nah, I just wanted to see if I could get you to do all the work." Lug smiled at his sister.

"I thought it was good of you to send the folks money from your first military paycheck so we could get our own pump. We didn't have to bum water from the neighbors after that."

"I had to, I didn't want you to break your back lugging those cream cans around."

"Yah, I really hated wash days. Ma had me hauling water all day when she washed clothes."

She got up and got a glass of water from the kitchen faucet. As she came back to the table, she said, "I've been talking to a spiritual leader about you. He wants you to come and see him. Don't forget to take him tobacco."

"That sounds like a good idea. I've been wanting to talk to someone," he said.

"What was it like in the war? You never talked much about it."

Lug stared deep into his black medicine water as if expecting an answer to scroll across. He trusted his sister but it was still difficult talking about the terrible memories.

His eyes retreated into his head as he told her what happened to him, what he did in the war. She later learned that this was called the thousand yard stare. His eyes looked like he was trying to see something that was that far away. The laugh lines were erased from his face.

"Sometimes I'd get so scared I couldn't get scared any more," he said, hunching over his coffee cup.

Judy touched his arm. Her face said she was ready to listen to her brother.

"One night they were shooting at us. No one was getting hurt. It got to be a drag ducking every time they fired. The gunfire wasn't very heavy, just a rifle round every couple of minutes. We didn't know if it was the prelude to a big attack or just one guy out there with case of ammo and a hard-on. We laid in our holes, counted the rounds going by and tried to shrink up inside our helmets. The bullets went by for at least a half hour. I counted 17 of them. The ones that went high made a buzzing noise as they went by. The close ones made a crack sound. First you'd hear the bullet go by then the sound of where it came from.

"I got tired of that shit. I crawled up out of my hole and just stood there. I wanted to see where the guy was shooting from. The guys in the next hole told me to get down but I was in a fuck-it mode. I didn't care what happened, didn't care if I lived or died."

Lug stood up to show his sister what it was like standing in the dark. He was leaning forward trying to see through the night. His hands clutched an imaginary rifle. Lug's head was swiveling back and forth as he looked for the hidden rifleman. He jerked as a rifle bullet came close to him. He turned his head toward the sound.

Judy watched Lug. She could feel her eyes burning and the tears building up. Using only willpower, she held the tears back. Judy somehow knew the tears would stop the flood of memories coming out of her brother. She waited.

"I finally saw the muzzle flash. I knew where the bastard was firing from. After he fired the next time we all returned fire. We must have shot 500 rounds at him. The bad guy didn't shoot anymore. We either killed him or scared the shit out of him. After the noise died down I started getting scared. I realized I could have been killed standing up like that."

He paused before speaking again.

"That shows you how dangerous a fuck-it attitude is. I guess I have been living my life with a fuck-it attitude."

Lug sat back down and reached for another piece of cornbread. He ate it silently. When he finished the cornbread, he lit a cigarette.

She touched his shoulder as she poured more coffee. Lug accepted this as permission to continue fighting the war. Judy sat down.

"It was really crazy at times. One time we were caught out in this big rice paddy. They started shooting at us. I was close to the front of the formation so I got inside the treeline quick. The bad guys couldn't see me. When I leaned over to catch my breath, I heard the snick, snick, bang sound of someone firing a bolt action rifle. The enemy soldier was firing at the guys still out in the rice paddy. I figured out where the bad guy was from the sound—snick, snick, bang. I fired a three-round burst at the noise. That asshole turned and fired at me. I remember the muzzle noise and the bullet-going-by noise happened together. I fired again as I moved closer. Through a little opening in the brush I could see what looked like a pile of rags, bloody rags. I fired another round into his head. We used to do that all the time—one in the head to make sure. The 7.62 bullet knocked his hat off. When the hat came off all this hair came spilling out. It was a woman."

Lug slumped at the kitchen table unable to continue his story. He held his coffee cup as if warming his hands. Judy sat there looking at him. Tears were running down her face and puddling up on the table.

Lug coughed and lit a cigarette. Judy reached for one of her own and Lug lit it for her. She got up to blow her nose and wipe her eyes. Judy was trembling as she came back and sat at the kitchen table. She wanted to cradle her brother but couldn't.

"Her hair looked like Grandma's hair used to look. Remember her long, black shiny hair? This woman had hair like that. I knew killing people was wrong somehow but this made it worse when it turned out to be a woman."

Lug was slowly rocking his head back and forth.

When it looked like Lug was not going to talk anymore Judy got up and opened the back door. She poured more coffee and sat there looking at him. He couldn't meet her eyes.

"Tell me how you got wounded, you never did talk about it. All we knew was that you had won a Purple Heart," she probed.

After a long silence, Lug answered.

"Ha, won a Purple Heart? We used to call them Idiot Awards. It meant you fucked up somehow. Standing in the wrong place at the wrong time, something like that."

Lug's shoulders tightened up as he began telling her about his wounds.

"I don't know what happened to my leg. It was a long firefight, lots of explosions. After it was over, after the medivac choppers left, we were sitting around talking about what happened. I looked down and noticed blood on my leg. I thought it was from the guys we carried in from the listening post. The pain started about then. I rolled up my pants and saw a piece of shrapnel sticking out. Doc came over and pulled it out. He bandaged it up and must have written me up for a Heart. I remember it took a long time to heal because we were always in the water of the rice paddies."

Lug was absently rubbing his leg as he told his sister about his wound.

Lug stood up and changed the subject. He didn't talk about his other wounds. He drained his cup.

"I gotta go, I think I talked too much already. I don't want you to think I am crazy because of what I did in the war. I'll see you at the powwow," said Lug, walking to the door.

As she looked at his back, she wished there was something she could do to ease his memories of the war.

"Wait a minute," Judy told her brother.

She lit some sage and smudged him with an eagle feather. He stood there with his eyes closed, palms facing out.

He thanked her and walked out the door.

While cleaning up after her brother, Judy remembered hearing the ads on TV for the Vets Center. She looked the number up in the book and called. Judy spoke to a counselor who listened. The counselor suggested an in-patient Post Traumatic Stress Disorder program.

The closest one was located in southern Minnesota. Judy got the address for her brother.

She went back to the powwow and found Lug standing on the edge of the crowd.

"They have a program for treating PTSD," she told Lug.

"Yah, I saw something on TV about PTSD."

"What did you think of it? What do you think about entering a treatment program?"

"It might do some good. I was talking to a guy who went through it. He said it helped him. It might be worth a shot," Lug said.

"I talked to a counselor after you left. She says you can come in anytime."

"How about right now? Do you think they are open right now?"

"Sure, they must keep regular hours."

When she saw him walking to his car, she thought it didn't take much to get him started.

Lug left the powwow and drove to the Vets Center. On the way he listened to Dylan singing "Blowing in the Wind."

At the Vets Center Lug found out he could enter the program in a couple of days. His stay would be about a month.

Lug talked to the spiritual man before he went in for the program. He remembered to bring him a package of Prince Albert tobacco and a pair of warm socks.

In talking with the man, Lug learned that veterans were respected because of the sacrifices they had made in the war. He told Lug he would pray for him. The spiritual man told Lug to come back and see him when he got out of the Veterans Hospital.

Lug went to see the counselor and she helped him fill out the paperwork. He thanked her and drove to his sister's house. He parked his car and went inside. Judy showed him where he could leave his car parked while he was gone.

Judy drove Lug to the brick hospital. Lug took his bag of clothes and walked up the steps. Judy waved from her car. Lug noticed that she was parked under an American flag as he turned and looked.

He walked into the building. The smell of disinfectant reminded him of the other official buildings he had been through.

Lug was ready for whatever was to come. Don't sweat the small shit, he thought.

Lug quickly learned that he was not the only one having trouble coping with the memories of the war. He felt comfortable talking with other vets who had similar experiences.

Living in the Veterans Hospital felt like being in the military again. He slept in a warm bed and ate warm food. Lug spent most of his time with guys his age who had been to Vietnam. His time was structured for him.

In the group therapy sessions they told war stories at first. After a while together they began to talk about feelings. Lug became aware of the fact that he was acting normal in what was an abnormal situation. He felt like he was leaving some of his memories at the hospital.

In spite of the camaraderie he felt, Lug was anxious to rejoin his community. He wanted to go home. Lug knew he would complete the program but didn't intend on spending one extra minute at that nice hospital.

While he was gone Judy was busy. She was making Lug a pair of moccasins. The toes had the traditional beaded floral design. Around the cuffs she stitched the colors of the Vietnam Campaign ribbon. She had called the counselor at the Vets Center to make sure the colors were right. It was green, then yellow with three red stripes, yellow then green again. The smoke-tanned hide smell came to her as she sewed.

The hardest part was going down in the basement for the trunk her husband had left when he went to Vietnam. The trunk contained the traditional dance outfit her husband used to wear. It had been packed away since he didn't come back from the war.

Judy drove to the hospital and picked Lug up when he had completed the PTSD program. Looks like he put on some weight, she thought when she first saw him.

She drove to the spiritual man's house. Judy was listening to a powwow tape while driving. Lug tapped his hand on his knee in time to the drum. On the way Lug told hospital stories. She could see the laugh lines as he talked about his month with the other vets.

At the house Judy waited outside while the two men talked and smoked. She listened to both sides of the tape twice before Lug came out. He had a smile and walked light on his feet. Lug opened the door and got into the car.

Judy drove toward her house.

"I've got that extra bedroom downstairs. You can stay there until you get your own place," she told him.

"Sounds like a winner, cornbread every day?" he asked.

"Nope, special occasions only."

"I might be eligible for a disability pension but I'd rather get a job."

"Do what you want to do," she said.

"Where are we going now?" Lug asked.

"We're going to a powwow. I got my tent set up already and I want to dance in the first grand entry."

"Okay, it'll feel good to see familiar faces again."

"Did the hospital do anything for you?" she asked.

"I think so but it felt better talking to the spiritual man," he answered.

When they got to the powwow grounds Judy drove to her tent. Lug perched on the fender when she went inside to change into her jingle dress.

Sure the hospital was nice but it felt better being here with his relatives, Lug thought. He breathed deep in the cool air. He could hear his sister's jingle dress begin to make sounds as she got dressed. He was trying to decide which food stand to start with when she came out.

"Tie this up for me, will you?" she asked.

Judy handed him the eagle fluff and medicine wheel. He used rawhide to tie it to her small braid. After she checked to make sure it was the way she wanted it, Judy said "Go into the tent and get your present."

"Okay," he said, leaping off the fender and unzipping the tent.

Inside the tent he saw a pair of moccasins on top of a traditional dance outfit. The colors of the Campaign ribbon on the moccasins caught his eye. He took off his sneakers and put on the moccasins.

"Hey, thanks a lot, I needed some moccasins," Lug told his sister.

"The rest of the outfit belongs to you too."

"Really?" He recognized the dance outfit. He knew where it came from.

"Hurry up, put it on, it's almost time for grand entry."

Lug put on the outfit and stepped out for the inspection he knew she would give. He did a couple of steps to show her how it fit. They walked to where the people were lining up. He laughed as he joined the traditional dancers. He saw his cousin who was a veteran.

Fuzzy was in Khe Sahn in 1968.

"Did you hear? They got a new flavor for Vietnam veterans," Lug told his cousin.

"Yah, what is it?" asked Fuzzy.

"Agent Grape," said Lug.

Both of them laughed at themselves for laughing.

Lug danced the grand entry song with slow dignity. He moved with the drum during the flag song.

When the veterans' song began, Lug moved back to join his sister. Both of them had tears showing as they danced the veteran's honor song together.

Jim Northrup

Sawyer, Minnesota

Jim Northrup's poetry, fiction, and non-fiction have appeared in many magazines and anthologies, including *Touchwood: An Anthology of Ojibway Prose, Stillers Pond, North Writers: A Strong Woods Collection, Aurora, Encompass, Rag Mag,* and *Frags and Fragments: Vietnam War Poetry,* and he writes a syndicated newspaper column, "The Fond du Lac Follies." The first collection of his stories is entitled *Walking the Rez Road* (Voyageur Press). He works as a roster artist for the COMPAS Writers-in-the-Schools program and a mentor for the Loft's Inroads Program in Minneapolis. Recently, his performances have been featured on National Public Radio and PBS. Northrup and his family live the traditional life of the Chippewa on the Fond du Lac reservation in northern Minnesota.

Adrian C. Louis

Pine Ridge, South Dakota

Verdell's View of Crazy Horse

Inside the post office a poster
displays new stamps: romantic Indian war
bonnets in hues never seen by our ancestors.

Outside, bruised and bumbling
unsika winos tread by with Hefty Bags
full of flattened beer cans.

On dilapidated Main Street
moans of Christmas carols curiously float
from Big Bat's Conoco Station and Mini-Mart.

In a frozen fissure on the uplifted pavement
an empty crack vial sleeps.
Grandfather! Can this plastic clue

to unhappiness be anything else but our own fault?
Despite the fact that the outside world
now haunts this nation with white man dreams,

it's really like my friend Verdell always says:
"When *Tasunke Witko* was murdered
that day at Fort Robinson

the last living free Indian died."

Halfbreed's Song

The idyllic intrudes briefly.
The playful Dakota sun burnishes
the hoarfrost on cedars
and dreams of winter are melting.
Kids are tight-rope walking
snow-packed streets to school.
A sudden warm wind gently shakes
the neighbor lady's clothesline
flock of red, white, and blue panties.
I pull out the snarls and braid
my burden of waist-length hair.
When I first left home
more than a quarter of a century ago,
I had a flat-top with wings.
I took a job in a Reno casino
making change for fools at the slots.
My sister has a photo of me from those days.
What a strange, muscular clown I was.
Striped, button-down shirt, Hush Puppys
and pressed corduroy slacks
and that goofy flat-top with wings.
No men wore braids back then
and I was ashamed of my Indian blood.
Grandfather . . . no shit . . . sometimes I still am.

How Verdell and Doctor Zhivago Disassembled the Soviet Union

"You are the blessing in a stride towards perdition when living sickens more than sickness itself."   - Boris Pasternak

Last year, before cruising to the warehouse
near the old Moccasin Factory,
Verdell and I stopped at the bootlegger
for a quick belt to cinch
his stomach full of fears.
He said the pint of rotgut whiskey
tasted worse than gangrene
but it did the job and choked silent
the raging world around him.
We meandered through tons
of remaindered and donated tomes,
a tax-deductible donation
to destitute savages, these boxed words
were stacked from concrete floor
to sheet-metal roof.
Buzzed-up and warmed by his whiskey,
Verdell came upon four cartons
of Pasternak's *DOCTOR ZHIVAGO*
and became transfixed by the bright red
fake leather covering.

But, I saw dead ikons of the past
in cardboard, and glory on the grandest scale.
Deep in Holy Mother Russia
marching through the bitter snow
I saw peasant armies mouthing
death songs while
not knowing where
their souls would go.

We lugged those four cartons of Zhivago
bound in leatherette to his puke-stained Plymouth.
That spring, without an ounce of shame
and some pride, Verdell related how
he had liked the Russian story,
but he said he ran out of firewood
during the last blizzard of March
and his hungry woodstove
vaporized Yurii Andreievich,
sweet Lara, and those eerie blue wolves
howling at snowbound Varykino.
Again and again, Verdell burned the books
until the cast iron glowed a deep, dark red
and the way he figured it, the heat
from his woodstove melted the glue
of the Soviet Union that spring.

Bonesinging

I.

Sometimes you grow tired of gnawing
old bones, those remnants
of a life lived in the ecstasy of rage
and sometimes you become a rabid
cur, angered and ravenous for bones
buried in forgotten locations
of your brain-yard.

II.

From sleep hills of horror
the thunderbird screamed
at your graveyard of dreams.
A spirit boy sobbed
for his sword-hacked mother
in a wail more nerve-wracking
than the Great Spirit's deathsong.
From Nevada to Dakota and back again,
lesser deities danced in violent aerial anger.
Spirits of rock, tree and water
silently prayed for the buckskin race
whose frozen mud eyes
were bled of their vision
of desperate
dancing.
Exactly one hundred years later
beneath the lone, stone pillar at Wounded Knee
blood flows from your ears.
Here, in this air, are the whispers
of hundreds of old men and women,
young boys and warriors
murdered under a white flag of truce.

III.
There is so much that you have forgotten.
America has always been blind to the past,
and because of this, it has no soul.
Last year when a Japanese company
wanted to buy the concession business
at Yellowstone Park, the yip-yap patriots
whined remembered hints of Iwo Jima,
Guadalcanal and Corregidor.
But nobody asked the trees their opinion.
Nobody asked the bears to share their feelings.
You're no bear or tree, but you know that
recently, a flickering red paper sun
has come to you in dreams.
It rises in glory between calm blue seas
and playful white clouds and the ghost
choruses of Hiroshima and Nagasaki whisper
every painful, shameful word man has devised.
You do not claim moral superiority
but some mornings when you awake
you smell barbecued children
and see molten puddles
of pregnant
women.

IV.
Summer came and you were back in Nevada
after six years of your latest lam.
The welcoming sun anointed your head
with holy, delirious sweat.
The dry Great Basin welcomed you home.
A trumpet-blast wind blew
singing sand past your exiled ears.
You felt as free as free could be
and jumped up and ran with dust devils,

singing and crying with pure Paiute joy.
You hyperventilated, purging your lungs
of all purloined blues.
You whirled like a stepped-on diamondback
and beheld the miracle-mirage
of no telephone poles as far as you could see.
The great cancer of technology was in remission.
You screamed *aiiiiieeeee* and jackrabbits dashed
into the sacred four directions.
The court jester coyote smiled and hooted
and whispered that H-bombs were dropped here.
You still remember the palsied earth, but you
remember one stronger earth pain.
In Nevada, until 1953, Indians were not allowed
out into white towns after dark.
Upon that soil where we'd danced
for thousands of years, somehow, your people
fell through the cracks in the Liberty Bell.
In Nevada, until 1953, Indians were not allowed
out into white towns after dark.

O Nevada, your sweet native land.
Your Nevada, deep cesspool of greed,
Welcomer of whorehouses, strip mines,
casinos and hydrogen bombs.
Soil where your ancestors are buried.
Land where Wovoka tied your Paiute people
to the mass grave at Wounded Knee.
Now you understand with your erotic heart,
those stories of Japanese soldiers
still marching to the Emperor's beat
on small islands a decade past V-J Day.
You know that when they were discovered,
some went joyously berserk,
weapons raised into a finality of defeat.

Some sat with their bowls of rice
and ignored the new ghosts
who had not been invited to dinner.
Others sat calmly collected
and with great relief,
they disemboweled themselves.

Bad Orange Sunshine Flashback

I came in from the wilderness, a creature void of form.
"Come in," she said. "I'll give you shelter from the storm."
                                    - Bob Dylan

It was late August in '67
when I purposely passed gas
and walked out of the office
because the shrink had skunk
breath and couldn't say something
immensely intelligent like
"If you objectify your plight
with the fatal interrogatives
then healing catharsis will occur."
I sucked down a small roach
and walked back up to the Haight
where I crashed with Noreen,
an artist who made boobs
out of plaster of paris.
When they dried, she spray-painted
them with red or green or blue
metal-flake paint
and glued a catseye marble
where each nipple should be.
Noreen's the one who
made me shave the hairs
around the shaft of my war lance.
She said it made me look slick,
all the more handsome.
I was young and knew
very little of split-tail ways.
Over the Sierras in the dry Indian
time warp I'd come from,
they were still running

the single wing.
Noreen was the first white woman I ever had
so I promised her that I'd see
a shrink after I freaked
on tab and a half of bad
orange sunshine one night
and shotputted twenty of her tits
out the window and onto Oak Street
where they exploded like milk
grenades on black asphalt.
"Far out, but either get some counseling,"
she said the next morning, "Or move out."
Well, I lasted five more weeks with her
in tit heaven but I never went back
to that shrink with skunk breath
and maybe blew the chance to nip decades
of angry-dick madness then
and there in the bud.

Just Another Suicide Note
for Patrick Stanhope

Six a.m. on this Indian reservation. I'm on the couch in my shorts watching The Weather Channel and drinking decaf. I let the dogs out and they hop off the porch, pee, then howl to be let in. This blizzard is two months early and it's not just a freak storm. It started the day before Halloween and has been going on for two weeks now. Dumb-ass leaves on my Lombardy poplars have frozen into lime-green popsicles and pull the branches toward the snowy ground. I haven't even winterized my car yet. I let the dogs in and get another cup and hear the old lady upstairs getting ready for work. When she leaves I will take a hot shower and pee and shave in the shower. Then I'll have a shot of whiskey and then go back to bed but not before I put on a rubber and pray for a wet dream in which Jack Kerouac returns from his bloated death and gives me a ghostly handjob and then introduces me to his buddy Elvis who will be dressed like Aunt Jemima and will cook me the yummiest cool daddy-o flapjacks or maybe some grits.

Fever Journal
Dakotah Territory: September 22, 1992

Bates, Bates, God damn Robert Bates,
last night I dreamed of you and
that time we jumped in that irrigation ditch
down past Campbell ranch and grabbed foot-long
carp with our bare hands and threw them on the bank
and then jumped on their heads until their
eyeballs popped out into the air
like the slimy green loogies
old men with bad lungs launched.

Bates, I thrashed around all last night like a carp,
sweating with endless chapters
of dick-chilling nightmares
of everything I ever did wrong.
Woke up on the couch at 2 a.m.
and watched PBS about JFK
and the "magic bullet" of Dallas.
Up this morning at 7 to cook coffee.
Fell back asleep waiting for it to brew
and woke by my woman at 10 calling
collect to ask if I wanted her to fix me
home-made chicken soup for dinner.
She said she'd be home from work
early to take care of me.

Bates, I'm so sick I'm peeing in a jar.
My man, when I was hiding from that terminal
Asian jungle disease twenty years ago
I forever lost track of you.
Hiding from my age twenty
days ago I had an affair
and my woman found out

and almost beheaded the old one-eyed
carp who swims around in my pants.
I'm sick. Sicker than I've ever been.
Oh, Bates, you old rat fucker.
At sixteen we sliced our wrists
and became blood brothers.
Made a solemn pact that when we married
we could screw each other's wives.
Bates, I don't know if you're living or dead.
Bates, I don't know if I'm
living or dead.

Ancestor Prayer

for Jimmy Santiago Baca

Cousin, if I shot coke or smack or crank,
my heart would explode or crumple
so I got no choice but to pray.
Ancestor spirits!
What is there I can recall
that will dissolve
this vortex of fever and fear?
Clorox won't do the job.
Ammonia won't shatter the nightmare
and I find no solace in the words
of the effete white poets
on my dusty bookshelves
who claim to be pals with Mr. Death.
Yeah, it's that funky Mr. Death sneaking
around my house in his droopy drawers.
I smell his liquored breath when I whisper
secrets into my cupped hands.
So, ancestor spirits! Hear me now.
Ancestor spirits! Heal me now.
Ancestor spirits! Heal all
us damn fool survivors.

Fever Vortex #5

One is punished most for one's virtues.   - F. Nietzsche

Green-clad cowboys
carrying silver knives
surrounded my gall bladder
and stabbed it to death.
I awoke in stitches
and fell back to gauze-soft sleep.
My hospital bed galloped through
morphine dreams of broken arrows
scattered in piles on the street corners,
on the dirt roads, in the back alleys
and the cottonwood valleys of my life.
The broken arrows whispered:
The road you are walking
has no beginning or end.
It's an old Indian curse.
Life's true beauty
is that it soon ends
so always make sure
you got clean
underwear on.

Nebraska Cowboys

A mid-February thaw startles
cows into dropping early
calves onto the muddy plains.
Even trees are tricked into budding.
Last week a cop in Gordon, Nebraska
murdered another Indian guy.
Shot him in the back and now
it looks like he'll get away with it.

When I was a kid you could always
tell who the cowboys were.
They always smelled like cowshit.
These days they wear nylon
panties under their jeans
and draw their guns as if
their redneck lives had meaning.
Damn this chapped-ass cowboy hell.
Damn this cow turd state of mind and
double-damn this verbal puke, this pain.

Some of What We Have Forgotten

*"You are fools, you die like rabbits when the hungry wolves
hunt them in the hard moon."*   - Chief Shakopee

There is so much we have forgotten.
There is so much we have forgotten.
Sometimes you want to scream . . .
Dream of possibilities,
shake that crystal orb and let snowflakes
lighten the darkness of your dying
heart within.

Sometimes you want to scream . . .
Ream the possibilities
and run buck naked
into a snowbank and explode
a blinding blizzard upon the world
by using nothing more
than your natural gas.

There is so much we have forgotten.
So damn much that I have forgotten.

Listen!
The cawing of crows
is the first sign of spring.
It is a sign of rain when horses
chase and kick each other.
When the owl calls your name
there is no cure for that.
In the meantime, remember this:
Take one teaspoon of sugar
and one drop of kerosene for a bad cough.
For earache, blow smoke into the ear.

For diarrhea, cook rice and drink the juice.
Or, drink a thin paste of flour and water.
Boils: pat raw bacon rind over them.
For warts, apply castor oil.
For ghosts, burn sweet grass.
Snake bite: slice a chicken through the breast.
Lay it over bite to draw out poison.
Chicken pox, measles: bathe in soda water.
Allergy: big leaves of sage will dry rash.
Listen, you can only pray for yourself
by praying for others.
This is important above all else.
There is so much we have forgotten.
Daisy: crushed leaves on bruise will relieve pain.
For a cut with infection: chew tobacco
and spit on the open wound.
Or, make a bread and milk poultice.
Cuts and tears: use turpentine.
Eczema: mix fat and rose petals.
Poison Ivy: the juice in the leaf
and stem of the Jewill weed.
Always share your food with others.
Never refuse when food is offered.
Whooping cough: use mares' milk.
For coughs: fry onions, wrap in flannel,
put on chest. Or, boil the bark
from the chokecherry tree and drink it.
The sap from the pine tree
makes a good gum.
The roots of cattails can be eaten
like potatoes or dried for bread.
The root of the soap weed (yucca)
is used for soap and shampoo.
Sunflower seeds can be ground into flour.
Dandelion stems can be chewed like gum.

Be strong for your woman;
not strong against her.
Brothers, be strong for your woman;
not strong against her.
There is so much we have forgotten.
Bulbs of the wild violet give
a good flavoring to soup.
Chew the root of the purple coneflower
for toothache, for bellyache,
to stop perspiration, and quench thirst.
Boil daisy fleabane for sore mouths of children.
Buffalo berries may be stored
up to five years without spoiling.
Buzzard oil is used for eye treatment.
The root of the gum weed
is boiled for liver problems.
Heavy drinking people
poison their children.
In blindness there is always an echo.
Heavy drinking people
poison their children.
In blindness sometimes there is a third echo.
Heavy drinking people
poison their children.
Jack in the Pulpit plant is good
for sore eyes.
Wild rose is brewed for eye wash.
If you see a ghost
that is what causes a stroke.
Sometimes a blind man is lucky.
Rosewater tea is good for sleep,
rest, and skin disorders.
Boil wild phlox for laxative.

The cawing of crows

is the first sign of spring.
It is a sign of rain when horses
chase and kick each other.

There is so much we have forgotten.

The Fine Printing on the Label
of a Bottle of Non-Alcohol Beer

Mickey Mouse, Minnie Mouse, Pluto too.
They're all movie stars at Disneyland.
Hey-ah-ah-hey-ya.
Hey-ah-ah-hey-ya.
　　　　- from "Mickey Mouse Song"
　　　　by The Black Lodge Singers

The Redskins are winning
and I'm on the couch waiting for
the second half of their grunt-tussle
against the Chiefs to begin.
By ancient Indian habit,
I dash to the fridge for more suds.
For four years running now,
it's been this sad, non-alcohol beer
for me and my liver.
As usual, I read the health warning
before I drink the ersatz brew.
On the bottle's label, it says:

My brother, you are pouring
this illusion down your throat
because you are an alcoholic child
of alcoholic parents and they
were the alcoholic children
of your alcoholic grandparents.
Before your grandparents,
your great-grandparents
lived without firewater,
without the ghost of electricity,
without the white man's God
in bow and arrow old time days.

Days of obsidian. Days of grace.
Days of buckskin. Days of grace.
Days of the war lance and the buffalo.
Days before your people learned
how to hotwire
the Great Spirit
with chemical prayers.

Vinny's Purple Heart

But it's too late to say you're sorry.
- The Zombies

I.

Man, if you're dead, why are you leading
me to drink after four sober years?
Vinny, can I get a witness?
I had a Snow White vision of the prodigal
son returning to America
that day of my final hangover.
I tried to clear the mixture
of cobwebs and shooting stars
from my brain with spit-warm
Budweiser, but the hair of the dog
just was not doing the trick.
I ended up pummeling myself
seven times that day and named each egg
white load for a Disney dwarf.
The first was Dopey.
The final was Sleepy, I think, or Droopy.

II.

Last year you scrawled a letter to me
about your first and final visit
to the Vietnam Memorial and how your eyes
reflected off the shiny black stone
and shot back into your brain like guidons
unfurling the stench of cordite
and the boy screams
of men whose souls evaporated
into morning mists over blue-green jungles.
You had to be there, you said.
That's where you caught the cancer, you said.

III.
Vinny. Tonight I had a dream of Mom's death
twenty years too late and now my eyes
will not close like I imagine the lid
on her cheap casket did.
I was not there when she died.
Home on leave from Basic Training,
you stood in for me
because I was running scared
through the drugged-out alleys of America,
hiding from those Asian shadows
that would finally ace you and now, now
in the dark victory of your Agent Orange cancer,
it gives me not one ounce of ease
to say fuck Nixon, fuck Henry Kissinger,
fuck all the armies of God and fuck me,
twenty years too late.

IV.
History is history and thank God for that.
When we were wise-ass American boys
in our fifth grade geography class,
we tittered over the prurient-sounding
waves of Lake Titicaca . . . *Titi* . . . *ca-ca*
and we never even had the slightest
clue that Che was camping out
en las montanas de Bolivia . . .
We never knew American chemists would
kill you slicker than slant-eyed bullets.

V.
Damn Vinny. My four sober years have squeaked
by like a silent fart and I'm on auto-pilot,
sitting in a bar hoisting suds with ghosts,
yours and my slowly evolving own.

When we were seventeen with fake I.D.'s,
we got into the Bucket of Blood
in Virginia City and slurped sloe gin fizzes
while the innocent jukebox blared
"She's Not There" by the Zombies.
Later that drunken night you puked purple
splotches onto my new, white Levis
and a short, few years into your future
this lost nation would award
you two purple hearts,
one of which your mother pressed
into my hand that bright day we filed
you under dry desert dirt.

Corral of Flame Horses

I.

That night in a high plains saloon
in Lawrence, Kansas when Crazy Horse
encountered the angry skinhead
he decided there was no need
to proceed procedurally . . .

Tasunke Witko wore red braid winds
and the caucasian chrome dome
lurched stinking drunk
against the bar and roared
"I can kick any Indian's butt."

Crazy Horse talked to me later
and said he wished
he had thrown a beer in the dude's face
or at least kicked him in the crotch
and shoved him down
on the ground, but he didn't.
He just grabbed his old lady
and headed out the door,
got in his car, pounded the steering wheel
and months later lamely joked to me,
said, "How could you scalp a bald man?"
Well, I had no answer. He hadn't told me
about pounding his steering wheel.
His wife had, so I had her.
Only the strong chiefs survive.

II.

THESIS STATEMENT: The romantic American West, that purple-
saged cowboy stage where upright and rugged individualists of
European descent carved out their God-given empires with sixguns

blazing never existed. All the Hollywood illusion, from Tom Mix to John Wayne to Robert Redford, is simply bullshit, political and mercantile at its core, as has been the bulk of serious literature devoted to the West. Thus, the question arises: what was and is the West? What is the essence of that land and spirit which constitutes the backbone of the American identity? *Beans.* Kidney, pinto, or Anasazi beans. *Beans* are the essence of the American West. Come here dear fathers and mothers of skinheads and take a deep Dachau whiff.

III.

SECOND ATTEMPT: THESIS STATEMENT. In his extended and excellent reading of the Lawrence situation, Crazy Horse immediately grasped that the "white west is not the Indian west" and here we have a theme which never runs through any of his wife's days with me. In a nutshell and beyond any conversation of quaint manifest destiny, primitivism, or cultural colonialism, for the Indian the West was simply home and not the *new frontier,* not the European model for a new hope. This perception is not new but is essential to understanding the West as depicted in much of American literature: in the primitivist and colonial eye, the European is complex, sophisticated, civilized; the native is the obverse, childlike, innocent, natural. This is the mechanism of control and children must be controlled, educated. It is why General Philip Sheridan could say in 1873 of the buffalo hunters, ". . . for the sake of lasting peace, let them kill, skin, and sell, until the buffalos are exterminated. Then your prairie can be covered with the speckled cattle, and the festive cowboy, who follows the hunter as the second forerunner of an advanced civilization."

IV.

Well, Lord, Lord, Lord Christ,
let's close out this account.
Today I heard a high plains descendant
of Sheridan shrug his red neck
and tell his sad joke about

"Indians being the end-product
of runaway slaves having had sex
with the buffalos . . ."
I know many Indians
who would be offended by that joke.
Myself, I'd be proud
if my father was a black man
and my mother was a buffalo.
I'd dance in my darkness and paw
the earth until my hooves reached
the molten core and the corrals
of the flame horses. I'd round them up
and free them and we'd gallop
together across the plains of eternity
giggling, farting, and flesh-baking
anyone who stood in our path.

For My Brothers and Sisters

Indians ain't got no sense.
Indians.
Indians ain't got no new cars.
Indians.
Indians ain't owning computers.
Indians.
Indians is Indians.

Mayo Clinic

My forty-fourth year
was mostly uneventful.
The days creeped
into weeks like green mold
on Wonderbread.
Then, one day in April
things changed.
I'd eaten mayonnaise
all my life but this
bright spring morning
I made the decision
to switch to Miracle Whip.
I strutted to the grocery store
and bought myself a medium jar.
I used Miracle Whip with tuna,
bologna, bacon and tomato,
egg salad, ham, spam,
thank you ma'am sandwiches.
I came to like the sweet taste,
but when the jar was empty
I went back to mayo.
Who says this shithole
is the land of the free?

Adrian C. Louis

Pine Ridge, South Dakota

Adrian C. Louis was born and raised in Nevada and is an enrolled member of the Lovelock Paiute Indian Tribe. He is the author of seven books of poems, including *Blood Thirsty Savages* (Time Being Books), *Ancient Acid Flashing Back* (Mother Road Publications), *Among the Dog Eaters* (West End Press) and *Fire Water World* (West End Press), winner of the 1989 Book Award from the Poetry Center at San Francisco State University. He has won many awards for his poetry including fellowships from the Bush Foundation, the Nebraska Arts Council, and the National Endowment for the Arts. Since 1984, he has taught at Oglala Lakota College on the Pine Ridge Reservation of South Dakota. His first novel, *Skins*, will be published in the spring of 1995.

WITHDRAWN